The Moon

Adria F. Klein

🔦 Dominie Press, Inc.

Publisher: Christine Yuen
Series Editors: Adria F. Klein & Alan Trussell-Cullen
Editors: Bob Rowland & Paige Sanderson
Illustrator: Michael Ramirez
Designers: Gary Hamada, Lois Stanfield, & Vincent Mao

Published by:

ᵱ Dominie Press, Inc.

1949 Kellogg Avenue
Carlsbad, California 92008 USA

www.dominie.com

ISBN 0-7685-0573-9

Printed in Singapore

12 13 V0ZF 14 13 12 11 10

Table of Contents

I circle the Earth
about every 28 days.

Each part of the circle
is called a new phase.

At first you can hardly
see me at all.

I'm just a small sliver,
so thin and so small.

8

Then I grow bigger and bigger each night,

until I am full and look round and shine bright.

But then I begin to get
slimmer and slimmer,

and the light that I shine gets
dimmer and dimmer,

until I have shrunk to a sliver,
that's all.

And next night, surprise,
I'm not there at all!

But wait! Is it true?
Do I really shrink and grow?

I might seem to change,
but it's really not so.

I'm just like a mirror,
and all that you see,

is how much light from the Sun
falls on me.

When you look through
a telescope, what do you see?

Bare rocky plains
people once thought were seas.

There are mountains and craters,
but nothing lives here.

I don't have the Earth's kind
of atmosphere.

Why don't you visit me?
Take a space trip.

All you will need
is your own rocket ship.

Blast off from Earth
and then pretty soon,

18

you'd be the first child
to land on the Moon!

Picture Glossary

crater: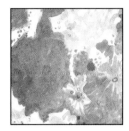

rocket ship:

Moon:

telescope:

Index